Rivers in the Desert:
Glimmers of Hope in Impossible Times

Katherine E. ST.

Published by KEYS Street Publishing Company.

ISBN: 978-1-948207-04-1

DEDICATION

For every soul that has ever found themselves in an
"impossible" season.

CONTENTS

ACKNOWLEDGMENTS

I want to thank my uncle, Rev. Dr. Moses Asamoah, Jr., for helping me realize gifts and talents that I was unaware of, for believing in me when I wanted to give up, and for reminding me that life can be "a lot," but, with God, nothing is ever "too much." This book is my version of "Thank God for Goliath." You showed me how. Thank you, Uncle Se.

Rivers in the Desert

Rivers… in the desert?

I dare not ask if it is possible.

The God who parted the sea,

Raised the dead,

Had over 5000 fed

With fish and bread

Ought not to be questioned…

About what is

"Possible"

Instead

I wonder

If I'm doing my part

To believe and declare in faith what I heard

The Lord say.

What's my part?

If not to

Keep the Word, and

Speak the Word, and

Eat the Word

Until my declaration becomes the seed

From which the Lord will cause the

Word to bear fruit in my life that is

Sweet?

Sweet

Like lemonade on a hot summer day

Sweet

Like hot chocolate on a cold winter night

Sweet

Like manna that came every day

Like rain in a drought

Like rivers. In the desert.

Isaiah 43:19

Belonging

Isn't it funny how

We've all experienced the phenomenon of

Feeling lonely while standing in a crowd?

Feeling like we are included but not?

Like

The adopted child, or

The gifted student, or

The one who is American but "not"?

Too this

Too that

Not enough this

Not enough that

Belonging here

And also belonging   there.

And so

Belonging

                            Nowhere

How is it that so many of us (...All of us?)

Have experienced the pain of not

Belonging

?

Love and _____

Have you ever had this feeling?

Like a vacation that you never want to end?

Like a summer night that is so full of life?

Like you could relive that day over and over and over again?

Like you could look into their eyes forever?

Like you could talk to them for hours?

Like if no one else ever came into your life, you'd be fine?

(In fact, you'd prefer it that way

Because what you have is so full that it feels like enough.)

Until...

It's not.

It's not what you thought it was...

And you find yourself having to say

Enough!

Enough of the complacency, the passivity

Enough of the imaginary scenarios you play in your head

Enough of the endlessssssssssssss wondering

What they're thinking

Why they said what they said

Why they ~~did~~ do what they ~~did~~ do

Enough!

Enough of the sleepless nights

Enough of the disrespect, disregard, dissonance

You're screaming, "I want peace!" but they can't hear you…

[They only want problems]

They only hear what they want to hear…

Do what they want to do.

So you had to make the decision

to leave.

Have you ever had this feeling?

Remember When

Remember when we went to that one place and did that one thing that one time?

It was so fun.

I remember thinking,

"Is this living?"

If so, I don't ever want it to end

Just want to replay the day

Over and over and over

again.

Remember when?

Remember?

Remember when we used to laugh until our ribs hurt and made up fun things to do on the fly and imagine where we'd be in 5, 10, 20 years?

What our kids would be like?

Who they'd look like?

What sports they'd play?

How they'd be best friends…

Remember when?

Remember?

Seeds (Not Today, Satan)

Oooh, I want to **so bad**!

REAL BAD.

Like what if I just…

Just for a second, you know?

Not all-in, just

A teeny tiny bit

Like

Just a bite?

No one is even here

I mean

Except for God…

Aaaaaaaargh

NO. Nope.

Not today, Satan.

Let me get up.

Let me call someone.

(No, not *them*. Someone else)

Let me:

- Go for a run.

- Go home.

- Go pray.

- Go do something else. Something *productive*.

Because the enemy is crafty

And I will be smiling in cne moment

And crying in the next.

Because it only takes a second

To fall.

And maybe. MAYBE

"No one else will know,"

But we all know

That eventually it will show

And EVERYONE will know

From the fruit

Of the seeds

That we're planting.

Because whether good or bad,

They will show.

And <u>everyone</u> will know.

What fruit do you want them to know?

Plant those.

Joy in the Mourning

"Misery loves company"

It's true… to an extent.

It's nice to know that you're not the only one going through it.

Same storm, different boat typa deal.

But it's also encouraging to see your tribe winning.

A glimmer of hope, if you will.

A sign that there is light at the end of the tunnel.

Or even *through* the tunnel.

But it gets hard when

You see others winning.

And you look at your life, and

You're not *losing* per se…

Just doesn't feel like you get your trophy yet.

But

Prizes imply competition

And

This isn't a race.

At least, not that kind.

So even when I'm crying,

I'm still smiling

Because I know that

I have a God Who never fails.

And though weeping may endure for a night,

Joy comes in the morning.

And I'll be okay.

Actually,

I'm okay right now :)

Dear _____,

I'm sorry. I didn't know it then, but my tone was off. My words weren't as loving as they could've been. I'm sorry for all the times that I made you feel small. That wasn't my intention at all. I guess I was in some kind of shock.

I'm sorry that I didn't have as much grace for you then as I do now. I'm sorry for not considering where you were. I was caught off guard, and I didn't know what else to do but tell the truth of how I felt. I didn't mean for that to make me lose you. I'm sorry.

I hope you can forgive me for the words that I used, for the tone that I chose. For every way that I hurt you, I am sorry. I hope you can forgive me. I hope we can be whole again, if not together, then individually. Maybe one day you'll be able to speak to me again. For real this time. I'll listen.

I miss you.

I love you.

Take care.

Et tu, Brute?

You think it'll never happen.

At least, you don't expect it to.

At least, you *shouldn't* expect it to.

But then, inevitably, as life goes on…

It does.

A kiss.

A knife.

Some money.

The throne.

Was it worth it?

Judas, was it?

Was it worth it?

Brutus, was it?

My heart is bleeding,

Wounded,

Heavy,

Hurting.

Why did it have to be

You?

Matthew 26:23 | Psalm 55:12-14

I Forgive You

I didn't like it.

At all.

You hurt me.

A lot.

I don't understand why you did that.

I told you I didn't like it.

I know I did.

I think I did.

I know you knew, either way.

And you left me with the pieces.

A contrast between before   and   after

And I... don't know what to say.

What I *do* know

Is that I'm tired.

And I don't want to be angry anymore.

And I don't want to give you power anymore.

I am not a victim anymore.

I forgive you.

And maybe you "don't deserve it"

Whether that indictment came from me

Or you,

It doesn't matter.

Neither of us deserved it when

Jesus gave His life for us

For us to know love

And peace

And forgiveness.

So.

Even though,

By natural standards,

You don't deserve it,

I forgive you.

He forgave me, so.

I forgive you.

I Forgive Myself

A picture. A video. A jacket.

A car. A fragrance.

Things that take me back to that one time when... I lost it.

Lost control

Lost my bearings

Lost myself.

And this resulted in words, actions, behaviors that weren't

Me.

I mean, it was me, but

It wasn't.

And when I think back, it hurts so much that I have to

Stop myself.

Why can't I let it go?

I have to forgive myself.

I did the best that I could do with what I had,

With what I was facing,

With what I was fighting.

I did the best that I could under the circumstances.

I did my best at the time. And maybe

It wasn't my all-time high, but

Nobody sees the internal struggles

Only

What I didn't do

Or didn't say.

But that's not fair to me.

I did my best...

I forgive myself.

Forgive Yourself

A movie. A song. A book.

A city. A color.

Things that take you back to that one time when… you lost it.

Lost control

Lost your bearings

Lost yourself.

And this resulted in words, actions, behaviors that weren't

You.

I mean, it was you, but

It wasn't.

And when you think back, it hurts so much that you have to

Stop yourself.

Distract yourself from what was done, what was said.

You can't seem to let it go

You have to forgive yourself.

You did the best that you could do with what you had,

With what you were facing,

With what you were fighting.

You did the best that you could under the circumstances.

You did your best at the time. And maybe

It wasn't your all-time high, but

Nobody sees the internal struggles

Only

What you did or didn't do

Did or didn't say.

But that's not fair to you.

You did your best.

Forgive yourself.

Tension

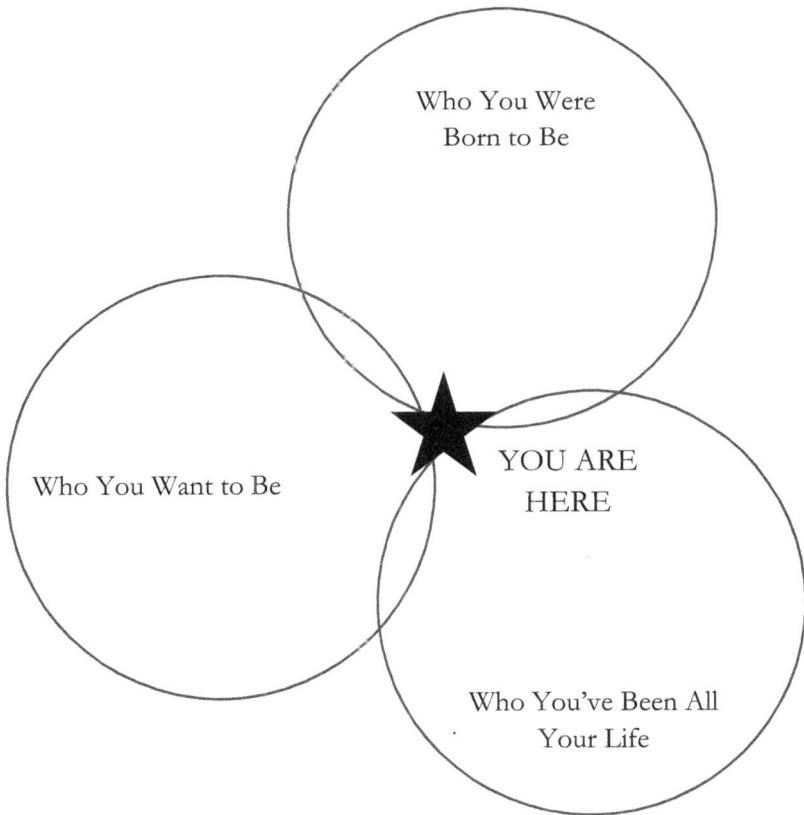

Foundations

Why did you make me like this?

Why weren't you there?

Why did you teach me that?

Why did you show me that?

Why did you hurt me?

Why didn't you protect me?

Why didn't you speak up?

Why   Why   Why   Why

Why.

How could you do that to me?

How could you think that was okay?

How could you leave me there?

How could you ignore my cries?

How could you?

How   How   How   How

How.

Mourning

Mourning is… whatever it makes itself out to be.

It can be silent.

It can be **loud**.

It can be feeling EVERYTHING.

Or.

Nothing.

Sometimes you don't realize its presence…

Until everything that you do

Goes back to that point.

That moment in time when you heard the news

When you were in shock.

When you were angry.

When you would do anything to bring them back.

When you realize that a second ago, they were there.

And then, a moment later

They were not.

They were   out of reach.

Poof.

Like vapor.

Gone

And then.

It's just you.

The sun rises and sets.

Life carries on

And you're just there.

You tell yourself to keep moving...

How do I keep moving?

Foundations II

Why did you make me this way?

I used to be so

Happy.

Unique. Content. Full of

LIFE.

But then.

One thing led to another and instead of love and peace

Fear and Pain began to shape and mold me

Fear would say,

"Be careful!

Watch out!

You can't trust anyone.

Fend for yourself.

Always have an exit plan."

And Pain would say,

"They *meant* to hurt you

You knew this would happen

Everyone is against you

It's not you; it's *them*."

And as a little one, I trusted you.

But as I grew,

I grew

Confused.

Is this the only way to be?

I began to question everything I'd known to be true.

I wondered

Is it possible to live | outside?

Outside of

The lies?

Because that outlook on life

Negates the power and sovereignty

Of God.

What if:

Love is saying,

"You're cared for.

I'm watching over you.

Trust Me.

I've got you.

You're safe."

And what if:

Peace is

Saying,

"That really hurt me.

I never saw this coming.

But instead of focusing on what you did to me,

I'm going to focus on what God is teaching me.

It's not you; it's Him."

I want to live THAT life.

The life in which I don't rely on myself,

But I put my faith in God,

Believing that He is able to heal me,

And keep me,

And guide me.

And I don't have to be

Scared.

I can be

Healed.

Because Jesus died to set me free

From the chains that refused to let me

Be.

The Lord filled the

E m p t i n e s s

That came from

Fear and

Pain and

Perfection and

Rejection and

Betrayal and

_____ [fill in the blank]

Thank You, Jesus.

Now that I'm at

Level Zero

I can finally

Build

Up

Genesis 45:8a

Solid Rock

Not my family.

Not my education.

Not my certifications.

Not my health.

Not the government.

Not my nationality.

Not my ethnicity.

Not my connections.

Not my money.

Not my intelligence.

Not my fame.

Not my gifts.

Not my talents.

Not my looks.

Not my retirement funds.

Not my bank account.

Not my trust fund.

Not my pension.

Not my insurance.

Not _____.

ONLY

Jesus.

Stronghold

[I] am not the leader.

I [don't] want to be the leader.

I don't [have] the confidence

[to] do it well without

[be]coming something that I wasn't meant to be.

I'm [afraid.] that I'll turn into a monster. Something other than

one who bears the image of [God]

How [is] it that I'm chosen to be in charge?

What's wrong [with] being number two?

How is it that you chose [me.]?

Shouldn't [He] be in charge?

How [will] this work?

Shouldn't I be the one to [help]?

How is it that you chose [me]?

I'm not sure I can [do] it well…

Is [it] my place?

It isn't… but it is… [right.]?

The Name God Calls You

Everybody has a name.

Or two.

Or a few.

There's the name that you're born with,

The names that your parents give you,

The nicknames that you get (some you love, some you hate)

There's the name you marry into,

Names that reflect your position,

Status,

Occupation.

And then.

There's the name God calls you.

Out of who you were.

Out of the things you used to do.

Out of who you used to be.

Abram was actually Abraham

Sarai was actually Sarah

Jacob became Israel.

You have a name.

A new name.

What's your name?

Sermon: The Name God Calls You. Pastor Moses Asamoah Jr.
Living Destiny Church | Norfolk, VA

Height Challenged

Be tall.

Be tall, but

Remember to look down when you talk to someone

Shorter than you.

But don't look at their feet

Look at...

Their shoulder, yes.

Oh. Which one?

Maybe right, maybe left.

It depends on the person, really.

Your neck might start to hurt if you look down too long,

Though, so

Be tall, but

Remember to look up sometimes, too.

Look up when you talk with someone taller than you

But don't look up their nose,

Even if you think they might need a tissue. Or some clippers.

Or some wax...

Maybe look away instead.

But not completely.

Like maybe

Up and slightly... to the left?

Or right.

Depends on the person...

But

Your neck might start to hurt if you look up too long, too,

So

Be tall, but

Remember to look straight most times.

Gotta see where you're going...

Your back might start to hurt 'cause you're squaring your

Shoulders all the time.

So

remember to look around sometimes as well.

But stay focused on where you're going

Except when you have to look up or down

depending on who you're talking to.

And don't forget that you're not the tallest.

(There are others taller than you, okay?)

Think you've got it?

Now go be tall.

Back to "Normal"

It's dark.

All around me, and I feel

Everything

And

Nothing

All at the same time.

Life doesn't feel real.

I wonder

If I'll ever

Get back to

Normal.

It feels like there's no going "back."

"Normal" is so far gone I can't even wish for it again.

It's gone.

It's gone...

It's _____

Hope Deferred

Hope deferred

Makes the heart

Sick.

Tired.

Heavy.

Sad.

Bitte- No.

I refuse to be

Ungrateful.

That ignores the faithfulness,

Goodness,

Gentleness,

Kindness,

Love

Of God

Proverbs 13:12

Anger

Why do you feel the need to talk to me

As if

I'm

Small?

Yet you ~~want~~ need... my help...?

I want to tell you about yourself...

Be mean with a smile like you were.

But

Man's anger doesn't work the righteousness of God.

So

Instead, I say,

"Have a nice day :)"

And scream in my head.

Take a nap in my bed.

Make sure I'm fed.

Then, try again

Tomorrow.

James 1:19-20

Breathe

Suffocating.

Air – trapped in my chest.

Sinking.

S

I

N

K

I

N

G

Emptiness. in the pit of my stomach.

I want out.

I want IT out.

Need to get it out.

Can't.

The words on the tip of my tongue.

Bursting - nearly - out of my chest.

Pushing their way up.

But not

Out.

What will they think?

What will they say?

How will I look to them now?

Will I still shine in their eyes?

Or will everything be… tainted?

I wanted to speak.

I wanted to share.

I wanted to tell you-

I want to cry.

I can't.

Maybe someday,

but right now, I can't

Breathe.

TRIGGERED

Fizz-ee-oh Logical. Response

(Physiological)

An alternate term for:

"When-your-body-knows-something-that-you-don't"

Or

Remembers what you wish you could forget...

OR

Remembers what you *actually* forgot. Wild.

You're fine, breathing, moving

LIVING.

One foot in front of the other and then

-Oop.

Wait a minute.

What was that?

What was... THAT?!

Sudden.

PANIC.

Heart rate:

RACING.

Mind: S P I N N I N G.

Gotta get out. Gotta get out. "Excuse me." *I've gotta get out. Gotta get out.* "I'm sorry, I have to-" *I've gotta get out. Can't get out. WHY CAN'T I GET-?* "MOVE."

I NEED SOME-

Air.

Outside.

Breathe.

Settle.

SCREAM.

Shapes That Speak | Language: Volumes

Rubik's cubes come in different sizes.

I expected to find the original 3 x 3 x 3, but

Come to find out, there are lots of different kinds.

There's 4 x 4 x 4, 5 x 5 x 5...

2 x 2 x 2...

One that's literally just one side (3 x 3 x 1)

Wildly enough, there's even a pyramid

But we won't talk about that kind...

Anyway,

Imagine thinking you had a 5 x 5 x 5

Then finding out that it's an original 3 x 3 x 3

Which is fine.

Except for when you realize

That it's the keychain size.

The King and Me

There's a King

Who has a Kingdom (obviously)

And I'm a servant in that Kingdom

Which means

That I do what the King commands.

Nothing more, nothing less.

I keep my uniform clean, and

I give Him reverence, and

I put away my feelings to do His bidding, and

I don't <u>ever</u> complain.

It's a pretty straightforward arrangement.

No confusion, no opinions.

He speaks, I move.

Case closed.

The King's Daughter

I have a Father (the King)

Who has a daughter (me, apparently)

So I'm a princess in His Kingdom (whaaat?)

Which means

That the King loves me

Forevermore, never less

He gives me new, clean clothes, every day, and

I give Him respect.

He lets me share my feelings with Him, and

Sometimes I complain, but

I always come back and listen.

It's an ever-growing relationship.

Sometimes I don't understand.

I ask questions; He usually answers.

And even if I don't like the answer,

I trust Him because

I know

That He loves me.

No matter what.

Case closed.

A Conversation with God

"I'm here."

It doesn't feel like it.

Especially when my heart is ripping out of my chest

and it's aching so badly that

I think something is wrong with me

and I just want it to

Stop.

"I'm here."

What's the point of any of this?

What is the point of life if we're constantly just hurting?

Will the pain ever

Stop?

It feels constant, never-ending

And yet-

"I'm here."

-You say You're here.

Also… constant.

And… Never-ending…

Hmm.

49

I guess I could try

Focusing on

You.

And as I focus on You,

The pain begins to dull

Dare I say

Heal.

And finally,

Instead of questioning

Or doubting,

I'm accepting

And aware

And grateful that

"I'm here."   You're here.

Taken for Granted

How crazy is it

That we often take for granted

Things that are so

Precious and

Sacred and

Sought after

?

It could be

Food or

Water or

Money or...

Peace

Safety

Family

Wisdom

Jesus.

To know Him

To see His hand in my life

To feel His love

To sense His holy, pure, filled-with-everything-that-is-good

Presence.

To hear His voice.

That comforts, directs, guides, shields, protects

Me.

How could I-

WHY did I ever

Take that

For granted?

God, I'm sorry.

Praise Him Anyway

God, it's dark...

I'll praise You anyway.

God, I'm scared...

I'll praise You anyway.

God, I don't understand...

I'll praise You anyway.

God, I'm confused...

I'll praise You anyway.

God, I'm frustrated...

I'll praise You anyway.

God, that hurt me...

I'll praise You anyway.

God, why did that happen?

I'll praise You anyway.

God, I'm angry at them...

I'll praise You anyway.

God, I'm angry at You...

I'll praise You anyway.

Even if You don't do what I know You can do,

I'll praise You anyway.

God, I'm _____...

God, they _____...

God, it's _____...

But I will

Praise You anyway.

Thirsty

There's a certain type of hunger that cannot be satisfied

With anything else.

Not fame

Not success

Not money

Not sex

Not even food.

There's a certain type of thirst that cannot be quenched

By anything else.

No amount of lemonade

Sweet tea

Alcohol

Or even water

Could be enough.

There is One who can fill that hunger, though.

He's the Bread of Life

And the one who tastes of this Life

Will never be hungry

Again.

There is One who can satisfy that thirst.

The One Who has Living Water

The one who drinks of this water

Will never thirst again.

It's kinda funny 'cause

He has this supernatural meal prepared for us

But

He's a Gentleman

So

Instead of barging in,

He knocks.

And patiently waits at the door.

Will you let Him in?

John 6:35 | John 4:14 | Revelation 3:20

My Keeper

Your Hand has always been upon my life…

Maybe, at first, it didn't seem like it

Because I remember when that happened.

And *that* happened.

And I wondered where You were.

Or why You allowed it.

But then again,

When I think of all the places I've been

And the things I've done.

And I consider where I could've been

Or what I could've done,

I realize

That You kept me.

You kept me from what I saw coming

But thankfully didn't actually come through.

You kept me from what I never could've seen coming

Which is good because if I'd seen it coming

I would've panicked.

And that anxiety might actually have led to it coming true.

A self-fulfilling prophecy.

Hmm.

In my ignorance, You kept me.

Why do I now think that my knowledge is what will save me?

It won't.

You are my God.

My Protector.

My Defender.

Thank You for being

My Keeper.

Psalm 127:1-2

No Turning Back

I have decided

To follow Jesus.

No turning back.

Love

Overwhelming

JOY

A flood of emotions.

G R A T I T U D E

Pure

Grace

Thank You,

Jesus.

Another Conversation with God

Hey, God

So.

Remember when You mentioned A, B, and C.

I was listening, You know. I think I'm ready for

D, E, and F. but like.

You haven't really said much else,

So I'm just wondering if, You know,

There's something that I'm supposed to be doing about that?

It's just that You were really loud about it for a time

But now it's like

Crickets, so.

Yeah, just let me know, You know?

I'm ready to do anyth-

"There are some other letters that I want us to

address first."

But what about the first three?

"Never mind those for now. I want you to work

on O, U, and... Y."

...

Uhhhhhh

That seems kinda random, like.

Is that code for something or...?

stares

stares

stares

Ooookaaaay... I mean, I think

A, B, C could be B-A-C.

Bac? Nah, missing a letter...

Maybe C-A-B.

Yeah, cab.

Is it-?

"Stop."

...

Sorry.

"I want you to put this first."

Put *what* first???

How???

Why???

smiles

"Exactly."

Cut Out the Noise

We often say that we want to hear God, but

It's hard to hear Someone when everything else is so

L O U D:

TV shows, movies, the news.

Music.

Fear.

Fear's cousin, Anxiety.

Expectations, disappointments.

Sometimes the Lord leads us into the desert

To answer our prayers:

"Lord, I want to hear You. I can't hear You."

So He allows situations that will force us into that place.

Isolation - not just away from people

But

Into a state of solitude

With Him.

Because we often need to cut out the noise

But either we don't know how,

Or

We don't really want to.

Because cutting out the noise is a sacrifice.

What do you want more:

Your comforts

Or

His voice?

Yet Another Conversation with God

Alright, so we've got

Y-O-U.

We worked on that assignment.

So, yeah, back to A, B, and C

I was thinking-

"When are you going to work on that dream I

put inside of you?"

...

Think I was tripping

Sorry, Lord, I think the enemy-

"That wasn't the enemy. I asked you a question."

Oop.

...

Why do we keep working on

Random things? We are jumping from

Place to place! All these random letters.

Hardly any words.

This stuff doesn't make sense...

"...Are you finished?"

...

...

...

Yes...

"Alright, let's go. I'll help you. Just start."

Okay.

Stars and Sand

Look left and you see

Someone getting something you asked for

Years ago.

Look right and you see

Someone getting something you asked for

Yesterday.

You look straight...

You tell yourself to focus.

Focus on what's in front of you.

Focus on what you do have.

Shut your mouth.

Be grateful.

You look up

With tears in your eyes

An ache in your chest

Fighting against the lies...

And you hear

"Stars"

And you see

Sand

And you breathe.

You cry and you sigh and you

Hold on

You learn

To hold on

Not to the promise

But onto the Promise Keeper.

You breathe.

And you move.

Forward.

Forward, toward

Him.

Genesis 22:17

The Mountain

It's really crazy 'cause

Level 10, Step 1 surely feels like

Level 1, Step 1.

Like.

I could've sworn I already dealt with this…

Already saw that tree branch.

Already saw those weeds.

Already smelled those flowers.

And yet,

We are here !

Again.

I am so far from the bottom, but

I'm not sure if I can see the top.

So I'm just here… putting one foot in front of

The other.

And wondering

If it gets any easier?

Or if we constantly always feel like

"Am I even moving at all?"

But

I realized that

That branch, those weeds, those flowers,

Were sharper, more invasive, and more pungent before.

Which must mean that the distance between me and them

Is increasing.

Which means

That I

Am indeed

Climbing

Up.

So.

I guess I'll keep going lol.

Hebrews 11:1

I have learned [and am still learning]

That when you're climbing a mountain,

Or fighting a giant,

Or walking on the sea,

You cannot focus on the terrain,

Or the opponent,

Or the waves.

You cannot worry about having all the right gear, or

Defending yourself from wild animals, or

How you'll manage to breathe high-altitude air.

You cannot consider the crowd, your armor, or

Your stature versus theirs.

You have to keep your eyes on the Lord.

'Cause otherwise, you will surely start to sink

Into doubt, depression,

Maybe even despair.

When you're climbing a mountain, you have to keep your eyes

Up.

Looking to Jesus…

Because then you'll realize that you can actually speak to the

Mountain.

And slay giants.

And defy the laws of gravity.

So

Look up.

And don't let anything create holes in your boat.

Desert Playlist

1. Just Wondering - V. Rose

2. Desert Song (Live) - Hillsong Worship & Brooke Ligertwood

3. Steady Me - Hollyn (feat. Aaron Cole)

4. Horizon - Hollyn

5. Be Alright - Evan and Eris (feat. Steven Malcom)

6. Better - Chastity (feat. Jane Handcock)

7. You Got It - Trip Lee

8. This I Know - Eris Ford & Evan and Eris

9. You Remain - Todd Galberth (feat. Chandler Moore)

10. Abba - Ryan Offer (feat. Ahjah)

11. Silence - JWLKRS Worship

12. Yes Song - KB

13. QUIET - ELEVATION RHYTHM

14. Known - Tauren Wells

15. 1,000 Names - Phil Wickham

16. Hills and Valleys - Tauren Wells

17. Here I Am - JWLKRS Worship (feat. Ashley Hess)

18. Fighting for Me - Riley Clemmons

19. Away - KB & Limoblaze

20. Loved by You - CalledOut Music

Rain Playlist

1. Didn't Know What To Believe - V. Rose & Najee Daniels

2. Give Myself Away - Chris Howland (feat. Eris Ford)

3. I Am Loved - Franchesca

4. I Am Loved - Mack Brock

5. Make Room (Live) - Community Music

6. Healer - Kari Jobe

7. You Revive Me - Passion (feat. Christy Nockels)

8. Present Helper - Marizu (feat. CalledOut Music)

9. Close - Roy Tosh (feat. Evan and Eris)

10. IN THE ROOM - Forrest Frank

Peace Playlist

1. Godsend - Riley Clemmons

2. The Breaker - Travis Greene

3. Loved by You - Riley Clemmons

4. Always On Time - Elevation Worship (feat. Bella Cordero)

5. Still God - Elevation Worship

6. Good Shepherd - Joe L Barnes

7. In the Name of Jesus - JWLKRS Worship & Maverick City Music (feat. Chandler Moore)

8. Thanks in Advance - Evan Ford & Evan and Eris

9. NO LONGER BOUND - Forrest Frank & Hulvey

10. Smooth - Jonathan McReynolds

11. Lowest - Evan Ford & Lashon Brown Jr.

12. Nothing is Wasted - Elevation Worship

13. Isaac - Hollyn

14. Thank You Lord - CalledOut Music

15. Who the Son Sets Free - KB & Scootie Wop

16. For the Good - Riley Clemmons

17. You Make Me Brave (Live) - Bethel Music & Amanda Cook

18. GOD IS GOOD - Forrest Frank & Caleb Gordon

19. HALLELUJAH - Forrest Frank

20. YOUR WAY'S BETTER - Forrest Frank

ABOUT THE AUTHOR

Katherine E. ST is an author, educator, and entrepreneur, among other things. She lives in Hampton Roads, VA and enjoys spending time with her friends and family. You can keep up with Katherine's latest adventures by following her on Instagram @Hey_LadyK.

* 9 7 8 1 9 4 8 2 0 7 0 4 1 *